The Kids' Volunteering Book

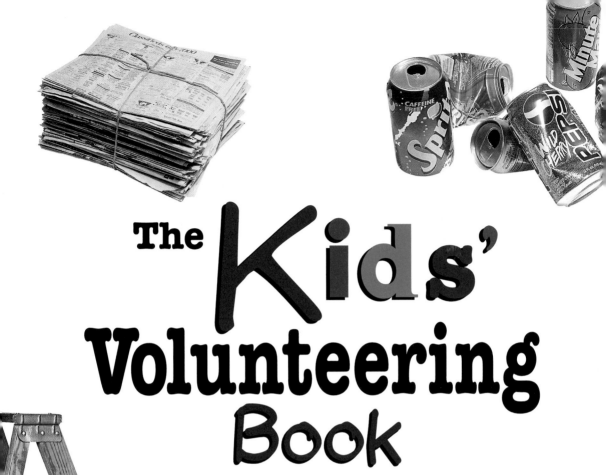

The Kids' Volunteering Book

by Arlene Erlbach

Lerner Publications Company
Minneapolis

To the children of the world
who give so generously of their time

The author would like to thank the following people and organizations for their help with this project: Ms. Nancy White and Ms. Jackie Geschickter at *National Geographic World* magazine; Gladys N. Bryer and Hymen Bryer; Diane Reckless and The Acorn Project; The Points of Light Foundation; Charles Halevi; and Felines, Inc.

The publisher would like to thank Jenna Browning, Dylan Crepps, Jade Crepps, Jessica Donovan, Kelly Donovan, Beth Jacobson, Sonia Jacobson, Cody Reisner, Chris Simondet, Jeff Sweetser, and Downie Winkler, who were photographed for this book.

Series Editor: Martha Brennecke
Series Designer: Zachary Marell
Photographers: Jim Simondet and Nancy Smedstad
Electronic Prepress: Mike Kohn and Jane Conway

Copyright © 1998 by Arlene Erlbach

Website address: www.lernerbooks.com

Library of Congress Cataloging-in-Publication Data

Erlbach, Arlene.
  The kids' volunteering book / by Arlene Erlbach.
    p.   cm.
  Includes bibliographical references and index.
  Summary: Presents some opportunities for young people to perform volunteer service, and briefly profiles some children who are volunteers.
  ISBN 0-8225-2415-5 (alk. paper)
  ISBN 0-8225-9820-5 (pbk.: alk. paper)
  1. Child volunteers—United States—Juvenile literature. 2. Young volunteers—United States—Juvenile literature. [1. Voluntarism.] I. Title.
HQ784.V64E75   1998
302.14—dc21   97-23356

Manufactured in the United States of America
1 2 3 4 5 6 – JR – 03 02 01 00 99 98

CONTENTS

73.780

Kids Are Volunteers, Too

Have you ever wanted to make a difference? Have you ever wanted to help someone, or be a part of an effort to change the world? If so, you're like plenty of other kids. Millions of young people, just like you, have volunteered their time and talents. They have helped people, animals, and the environment.

In this book, you'll meet kids who have reached out in many ways. Kids have worked at volunteer jobs. They've joined groups involved in a cause, or they've started their own

It's about time...to volunteer.

Earth watch

volunteer project. In some cases, one kid's effort was such a success that it launched a statewide or national volunteer organization.

Whatever any volunteer accomplishes, he or she is involved in something very important. Each volunteer makes the world a better place, somehow.

Volunteering not only helps make the world a better place to live, it helps you, too. When you volunteer, you'll learn more about yourself. You'll experience new situations and gain new skills. You'll meet new people and make new friends. Most of all, you'll feel good about yourself for making a difference in the world.

First let's meet some kids who have volunteered. Then you'll learn ways to start volunteering yourself.

two

Meet the Volunteers

Storyteller

Volunteer: Galen Dell

Galen became involved as a volunteer storyteller while raising money for kids with AIDS. He was selling candy for an AIDS charity, and he walked into a children's bookstore.

"The owner asked me if I'd like to baby-sit for her son at the store during the store's preschool story hour," Galen says. "So I did. I liked the story hour so much, I asked the

Galen and two fans, Neil and Graham

Illustrations from *Agassu: Legend of the Leopard King* by Rick Dupré, published by Carolrhoda Books.

owner if I could tell stories, too." Galen has been a regular storyteller ever since.

Sometimes Galen reads to the preschool kids. Sometimes he tells them funny stories or poems he has made up himself. First he reads or tells stories, then he has the kids act them out.

"Once we kept acting out *The Lion King* over and over again," Galen says, "because one four-year-old boy loved the story so much. I got tired of it," Galen admits.

Most of the time, Galen enjoys volunteering at the bookstore. He also feels that his work there is important. "The story hour entertains little kids," he says. "It opens their minds to all kinds of imagination, and it encourages them to enjoy books."

When Galen returned to school in the fall, some of the kids missed him. But he still worked at the store on weekends. Then Galen's fans were able to see him on TV, when he began appearing on a local cable program. On the show, Galen and the bookstore's owner discuss children's books. Galen doesn't get paid for that either, but he always enjoys it.

And what about the AIDS candy drive? Galen collected $456—more than anyone else. "I guess I just love doing things for people," Galen says.

IRAN and played at Grandpa's farm, GREENLAND so plush and full— I fed the pigs and milked the cows and rode on Istanbul.

Clowning around: Heather & Dad

Clown

Volunteer:
Heather Strange

Heather volunteers by clowning around. She brings joy and laughter to hundreds of people. Heather is Lovehart the Clown, who entertains regularly at the Houston Shriners Hospital and other organizations for physically and mentally challenged children and adults.

Heather knows exactly what it's like to be physically challenged. She has spent much of her life battling cerebral palsy, a disease that affects coordination. But if it hadn't been for the disease, Heather may not have become Lovehart.

When Heather was in the hospital for surgery on her legs, medical students dressed as clowns came to cheer her up. Heather loved their act and decided to become a clown someday, too.

Heather and her dad enrolled at a professional clown school in Houston, Texas. At clown school, Heather learned magic tricks, juggling, and how to play jokes on people. She learned how to put on clown make-up and dress like a clown. So far, Heather has been the school's youngest student. She's

one of the youngest clowns in the country.

Soon after clown school graduation, Heather began performing regularly at the Houston Shriners Hospital. All the patients, from toddlers to teenagers, love Heather and her act.

"Besides making people laugh, my act proves to kids that you can do anything in spite of a disability," Heather explains. "And I like coming to the hospital as someone who can help people, not as a patient."

Heather also performs each year at the Houston Rodeo Parade. A special block is set up for mentally challenged spectators, and Heather does her clown act for these people during the parade. At Christmas, Heather's dad dresses as Santa and she puts on her elf costume. The two of them perform at a local holiday dance for people with disabilities.

Heather on parade!

Heather isn't sure what she wants to be when she grows up. Not a clown. She'd like to be president of the United States, a veterinarian, or a zookeeper.

Day Camp Counselor

Lauren

Volunteer:
Lauren Tortorice

Lauren believes she was hired as a volunteer day camp counselor because she was well qualified, not because of her age. Lauren's the youngest junior counselor the camp has ever had on its staff. She was only 10 when she started volunteering. "I know first aid and CPR, and I have lots of experience baby-sitting for my younger cousins," Lauren says.

Every day during the summer, Lauren works with kids ages 6 through 11. She doesn't get paid for her work, but the town that sponsors the day camp gives her a free pool pass. "At first it was hard for the kids to get used to me being so young," Lauren says. "I got doused the most, on the days that the kids played with water balloons."

Lauren loves working with kids of all ages. "I enjoy showing them how to do things," she says. "I'm pleased when they can learn something new. I look back at the last two summers and feel good about how I spent my time."

Some of Lauren's duties involve refereeing games like Red Rover, Mother May I, and Red Light Green Light with the younger kids. She plays kickball and softball with older children.

"I always make sure not to play my best," Lauren says. "I want other kids to have a chance to win."

The volunteer counselor job will also prepare Lauren for her future career. She wants to be an elementary school teacher someday, and Lauren is already getting lots of experience with kids.

Josh, Joanne, Angela Burgess, and Margo Suzara (front)

Teachers' Aides

Volunteers: Joanne Zimmer & Josh Putt

When Joanne and Josh became volunteers at Chicago's Malloy Center for Children with Special Needs, they had different reasons for wanting to volunteer.

"My mom's friend's mom was a teacher at the center and told me it was fun," Joanne says.

"I have a friend with slurred speech," Josh explains, "so I know what it might be to be different. I thought it might be rewarding to work at the center."

Some of the children at the center had visual or hearing problems. Other students were mentally challenged or needed wheelchairs and walkers. Most of the children Josh and Joanne worked with were about the same age as Josh and Joanne—12 years old.

"The first few days I felt sorry for the kids," Joanne says. "Then I realized that they have strengths and weaknesses just like anyone."

"It didn't take me long to get used to the kids," Josh says.

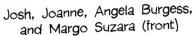

"They really appreciated us being there."

Josh and Joanne helped on field trips. They took the kids to restaurants, the botanical gardens, and the beach. The kids even made pizza and spaghetti together in the school's kitchen.

Josh left for camp a week before the summer school program was over. He was disappointed that he missed the party that ends each summer session. But both he and Joanne returned to sing Christmas carols in December.

The experience at the center has meant a lot to Joanne and Josh. They both enjoy helping and feel they've learned from it.

"The most important thing we've learned," Joanne says, "is these kids have the same feelings anyone else has. They aren't much different from anyone." Josh and Joanne strongly agree about that.

15

Disaster Relief & Landscaping

Volunteer:
Josh Gibbs

One summer evening, tragedy struck Josh, his family, neighbors, and friends. In a matter of minutes, Hurricane Andrew destroyed hundreds of homes in their area of South Miami, Florida. Josh lost his own house.

The Scouts help out.

After the storm, Josh wanted to help repair his community. He decided to rebuild something that everyone shared—Monkey Jungle, a zoo that's a popular Florida tourist attraction.

Monkey Jungle is an unusual zoo. People walk through areas enclosed with wire fencing to observe monkeys, chimps, and gorillas, that are free to roam. Monkey Jungle is also a park in South Miami where people often picnic.

Three generations of Eagle Scouts: Josh's grandfather, Josh's dad, Josh

Although the animals at the park survived the storm, the park's trees and plants were destroyed. Josh decided to help restore the park by laying mulch—a layer of wood chips or other material that protects the soil.

Laying mulch over a whole park is a big job. Josh knew he'd need lots of help, so he decided to involve his Boy Scout troop. The project could qualify him for the highest honor a Boy Scout can achieve, the Eagle award. And Josh would receive the help he needed, since troop members must support each other on their Eagle projects.

Josh, seven other troop members, and Josh's dad worked at the park for 12 hours in the hot Miami sun, while the resident monkeys entertained them.

Some monkeys stole mulch and played with it. One gorilla decided he didn't like Josh's friend, Darryl. Every time Darryl walked past the gorilla, the animal spat at him.

In spite of the gorilla problem, Josh's project proved to be well worth it. After his hard work, the park could be used again—and Josh received his Eagle badge.

Fundraiser for a Friend

Volunteer:
Becky Streifler

Becky has a brainstorm...

When she was in fifth grade, Becky Streifler organized a group of 15 classmates to raise money for another child's leukemia treatment. Becky and her classmates raised over $20,000 for Amri Aloni, a boy their own age who lives in Israel.

Becky first heard about Amri's illness when his parents wrote a letter to Becky's mother. He'd be coming to the United States for a bone marrow transplant, which is very expensive. It wasn't something that Amri's family, or most families, could easily afford. They wondered if Becky's family knew of a way to raise the money.

"I was shocked and scared to hear about somebody my own age being so sick," Becky says. "So I organized my friends to figure out a way to help him." Becky called the group Kids Who Care.

The group decided to hold a garage sale. Becky and her friends posted flyers about the garage sale around their town and at school. Becky's dad called a local radio station to broadcast Becky's organization. Local newspapers and a TV station also featured Becky and Kids Who Care. Soon Becky began receiving donations through the mail.

$10.00

...and she's in business!

"Money came from the most surprising places," Becky says. "One day I was walking down the street, and a man in a sports car stopped and gave me a $100 bill."

Between the garage sale and the donations, Becky and Kids Who Care raised $22,000. Becky had no idea they'd raise so much money. She was just happy to help someone her own age who was sick.

With the money the kids raised, Amri had a bone marrow transplant. The treatment was a success. When Becky visited Israel the next summer, she saw Amri. She also found a new volunteer project at a center for disabled athletes. So while Becky was in Israel, she didn't spend most of her time sightseeing or shopping, like most visitors do. Becky spent most of that summer in Israel teaching kindergartners to swim.

Helper at a Cat Shelter

Chris and Precious

Volunteer:
Chris Lawrence

"I've loved cats all my life," Chris Lawrence says. "I have two of my own, Leo and Corey. Working at the shelter gives me a chance to help cats that aren't as lucky as mine."

The Felines, Inc., animal shelter is home for over 100 otherwise homeless cats. When Chris is there, he brushes the cats and plays with them. He changes their boxes and feeds them, too. The shelter refers to these duties as giving TLC—tender loving care.

Chris also helps the shelter with its fund-raising events. He collects money at the shelter's rummage sale every month and at their annual Christmas bazaar. "Sometimes I even donate my old toys and clothes to the monthly rummage sale," Chris says. But what he enjoys most is the time he spends with his four-footed friends.

As much as Chris likes his job, it has certain hazards. Sometimes he gets attached to a cat and wants to take it home. His mom thinks that two cats are plenty for one house.
"There was one cat

named Bart that hung around me a lot," says Chris. "I loved to play with him. I missed him when somebody adopted him, but I'm glad Bart found a home."

Then there was Alex, a cat at the shelter that got sick and died. "Alex was really special,"

Eric, LeoLin, and friends

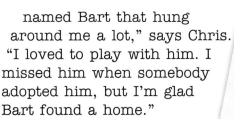

Chris says. "Everyone at the shelter loved him."

Chris is such an enthusiastic volunteer that he's been put in charge of the shelter's new Junior Volunteer Program. He goes to the shelter's board meetings, and he's in charge of recruiting and training other kids as volunteers.

One of Chris's recruits is his best friend, Eric Bevolo. Eric loves cats just as much as Chris does. Eric and his mom sometimes help out homeless cats in their own neighborhood. They also have two cats of their own.

Another junior volunteer is LeoLin Bowen, a girl who doesn't have any pets. To LeoLin, volunteering at the shelter is important because it gives her a chance to be around cats while helping them.

Chris realizes that the shelter serves the needs of both cats and cat lovers like himself. He says he won't ever tire of cats. When Chris grows up and has a place of his own, he wants to own at least seven cats.

Socks Across Tennessee

Volunteer: Ryan Rigney

Photograph by Leroy Munsey

Ryan sends his socks to shelters.

Ryan Rigney was inspired for his volunteer project by TV programs and the news. "I'd seen lots of programs about the homeless," Ryan says, "and I wanted to help them."

At first Ryan thought he'd use the $100 he'd received for Christmas to buy coats for homeless men. But he soon found out that his money wouldn't go far that way—Ryan would only be able to help a few people. He wanted to do more than that.

While shopping at a flea market with his mom, Ryan got an idea. His $100 could buy 200 pairs of socks at 50 cents a pair. Ryan bought the socks, and he and his family delivered them to Nashville's Union Mission, a homeless shelter. Ryan and his parents also stayed for the afternoon and helped serve dinner to mission residents.

Ryan's project was such a success that he entered *USA Today*'s National Make a Difference Day contest, along with 68,000 other entrants. Ryan won a runner-up plaque and $250. He used that money to buy more socks for people in need. Ryan gave those socks to other organizations, including a shelter for abused women and children.

Ryan's project didn't end in Nashville. A local sock company donated a truckload of socks—thousands of pairs—to Ryan's cause. Ryan had to store the socks in a warehouse. Then Ryan ordered telephone books from all of Tennessee's major cities. He looked through the phone books for places that serve people in need, and he sent them socks. Ryan paid for the warehouse and shipping with money he earned from mowing neighbors' lawns.

Ryan met a Miss Teenage Tennessee who told people about the socks as she traveled. A musical group spread the word about Ryan's socks, too. Tennessee's Senator Fred Thompson offered to take a box of socks to Washington, D.C. And when Ryan and his family vacationed in the Bahamas, they took along a box of socks.

Wherever Ryan's socks end up, the project fuels Ryan's belief in giving. "It doesn't matter how old you are—you can still make a difference."

What happens when Ryan runs out of socks? Every so often, a worker from the sock company calls him to see if he needs more. They've agreed to give Ryan more socks whenever his supply runs out.

TREE MUSKETEERS®

A national network to promote environmental awareness started with one tree planted by a Brownie troop. The club sprouted and grew into TREE MUSKETEERS.

In 1987 an El Segundo, California, Brownie troop felt bad about using paper plates and cups on a campout. They'd used paper because their campsite didn't offer enough water to wash nondisposable items. So after they returned to their hometown, the troop planted a sycamore tree. They had seen environmental problems firsthand, and they wanted to give something back to the Earth.

The original TREE MUSKETEERS: Brownie Troop # 91

This first tree planting branched out to become a local Arbor Day celebration. Thirty trees were donated for planting, and the event drew a crowd of 150 people. Each year since then, Arbor Day has been an important holiday in El Segundo.

Over the years, TREE MUSKETEERS has planted more than 700 trees. But that's not all the group has done to help the environment. Tara Church, one of the founders, organized one of the group's biggest projects: the National "Partners for the Planet" Youth Summits, which brings together hundreds of kids. No adults can attend unless a kid goes with them.

TREE MUSKETEERS was the first nonprofit organization in America to be run entirely by kids. Five adults and 13 kids serve on the board of directors. The adults are really only there to sign contracts that the kids have already made. The kids even hire their own employees.

President Clinton presents the Volunteer Action Award to Tara Church for TREE MUSKETEERS.

The organization has received more than 100 awards. One award was MasterCard's Master Planters' award, given to past board president Sabrina Alimahomed when she was only 14. It was presented at the National Urban Forest Conference. Another year, TREE MUSKETEERS won the President's Volunteer Action Award.

What do the group members think about their fame and what they've accomplished? "It's time for kids to do something about the environment," says Zoila, a youth employee.

Kids Konnected

Kids Konnected (Jon second from left)

Volunteer:
Jon Wagner-Holtz

When Jon Wagner-Holtz's mom got cancer, it was hard on the whole family. It affected Jon, his dad, and his sister, too. Jon's mom often felt sick from the medication she took. Her hair, eyelashes, and eyebrows fell out. Some of Jon's friends thought they could catch cancer from him. They even teased Jon about his mom being bald.

Jon decided to do something for other kids whose parents have cancer. "It's scary when a parent is that sick," Jon explains. "Kids need friends who understand."

So Jon started a friendship network for kids whose parents have cancer. He proposed his idea to the local chapter of the Susan Komen Breast Cancer Foundation. Dr. Dava Gerard, the center's president, liked the idea a lot. So did the Orange County Jr. Women's Club, and the club decided to fund Jon's project. Jon called his group Komen Kids at first. A few years later, the organization became a nonprofit corporation known as Kids Konnected.

Kids Konnected hooks up kids with a buddy they can talk to about their experience with a parent who has cancer. Jon writes a monthly newsletter for all Kids Konnected members. His local chapter has monthly meetings that involve discussion groups with a therapist and activities just for fun. His chapter's first meeting ended with a trip to Disneyland.

Jon speaks out for Kids Konnected to a group of 10,000 people.

Jon's efforts have earned him a lot of attention. He received an award from *Sports Illustrated* as Good Sport of the Year, and there have been two TV specials about Jon's work—a 4-minute documentary on the Disney Channel, and an 11-minute documentary on Nickelodeon. Jon has also been interviewed on two daytime talk shows and has met former President Ronald Reagan.

Kids Konnected has grown to include over 5,000 kids in 18 chapters worldwide. Jon's success with Kids Konnected has also inspired a group called Karen's Kids. This is a support group for kids who have lost a parent to cancer.

What does Jon think of his success? "In a situation when a parent has cancer, kids need to do something for kids," he says. Jon has most certainly done that.

Making music: Shamonda, Rochelle, Ola, Jasmine, Ronnika (left to right)

The Express Yourself Club

Volunteers: Jasmine Tyler, Ola Oyinsan, Rochelle Rupert, Ronnika Rupert, Shamonda McCorley

Lots of girls start clubs in elementary school. But few girls have a club like the one started by Jasmine, Ronnika, Shamonda, Ola, and Rochelle. Their Express Yourself Club performs music for people in nursing homes.

All the girls play musical instruments. Among the five of them, they play two clarinets, a flute, a violin, and a piano. Ola thought it might be fun to visit a nursing home. She suggested the East Grand Nursing Home, because it had the biggest picture in the Yellow Pages.

The girls' first performance at East Grand was on a Sunday in November. The girls performed solos and played together. They demonstrated dances. They also gave a plant to the home's oldest resident. They spent the rest of the day helping residents by pushing wheelchairs or offering arms for support.

The girls returned to the nursing home before Christmas. The activity director gave the girls names of residents whose families didn't visit often. The girls filled boxes with items such as toothpaste, shaving cream, nail polish, cologne, and shampoo. The girls' moms and their friends donated the items to the club's cause.

In addition to performing at the nursing home, some of the girls have performed at a children's hospital, where they gave out balloons. When they performed at a women's club, the club gave the girls a $75 donation. The girls split the money, and they each gave their part to their favorite charity.

When the Express Yourself Club entered and won the *USA Today* Make a Difference contest, they donated the $250 prize money to the Child Care Coordinating Council of Detroit–Wayne County. This organization pays for baby-sitters during emergencies, so that families who can't afford a baby-sitter won't leave their kids alone.

For Jasmine, Ronnika, Shamonda, Ola, and Rochelle, the Express Yourself Club isn't about winning money. "The club started as a way to express ourselves, have fun, and help other people," Jasmine says.

International Linen Drive

Left to Right: Reid, Hilary, Meghan, Matthew

Volunteers:
Meghan O'Connor, Reid Mammoser, Hilary Wiseman, Matthew Raidbard

How would you like to collect and pack 18 boxes of linens to be sent to a part of the world you may never see? The kids at the Niles Township Jewish Congregation in Illinois did just that. They gave an entire afternoon to sort and pack pounds of towels, sheets, and pillow cases. Then they sent the linens to a children's hospital in Lima, Peru.

The whole linen drive project took about a month. It began with the kids collecting towels, sheets, pillow cases, and blankets from friends, neighbors, relatives, and members of their congregation.

"The items didn't need to be new," Meghan explains. "They could be used and even torn." The hospital could use linens in any condition, because all the items could be recycled somehow. A torn towel could be made into a washcloth. A large damaged sheet for a queen-size bed could become a single sheet for a hospital bed. "The hardest thing was

explaining to people that the items didn't need to be brand new," Hilary says.

People gave items besides linens, such as crutches and walkers. A hotel donated bags of soap and shampoo. The donated items nearly filled the synagogue's youth office.

To support the kids, the synagogue sponsored events like a skating party and bowling party where kids got a dollar off admission if they brought linens. This encouraged all the synagogue's kids to become more involved in the project.

"I passed out flyers and explained the project to people," Reid says. "But near the end, I heard so many kids complain about spending a Sunday packing the linens, I wondered if anyone would show up."

But the last day of the project, 35 kids helped pack. The synagogue shipped the boxes to Florida, where the Peruvian Navy picked them up and sent them to the hospital.

"I felt great helping other kids," Matthew says. "But I was disappointed, too. I got sick the day we packed the boxes and couldn't help. I did get to bring in linens, though."

Hilary and Meghan brought the most linens of all. They each lugged in two garbage bags stuffed with sheets, pillow cases, and towels.

Choosing a Way to Help

You can't change the entire world—nobody can. But you can make a difference. There are thousands of ways to volunteer.

Maybe you already have an idea of what you'd like to do. Even if you're not sure what suits you best, just choose one way to volunteer, then try it. If you choose something that doesn't fit, you can always try something else.

Of course, you want to become involved in something you really care about. No matter how popular a cause might be and how many of your friends are involved in it, your work won't be rewarding to you if you're not interested in the cause. It's also important to choose something you're good at and something you enjoy.

Nail down your cause.

Think over the questions below before you get started on any volunteer project. They may help you decide on the project that's best for you.

FIRST QUESTIONS:

- **What means a lot to me—animals, the environment, elderly people, needy people of all ages, or little kids?**
- **What needs to be changed that I can do something about?**
- **Do I like to work indoors or outdoors?**
- **Would I rather work directly for an organization or design a project of my own?**
- **Would I rather work by myself or with a group of kids?**

Types of Volunteer Work

Most volunteer work falls into certain interest categories. Here are the most common categories of volunteer work and some ideas of what you can do to help. Many of the organizations mentioned have their phone numbers and addresses listed in the back of this book.

ANIMAL-RELATED

Are you a pet lover? Work at a local animal shelter. Offer to walk an elderly neighbor's dog.

If nondomestic animals interest you, contact the National Audubon Society or Defenders of Wildlife.

CULTURAL

Do you enjoy going to museums? Sign up to volunteer at a local museum. Do you and your friends like to sing, dance, or play an instrument? If so, you could perform together at a home for the elderly or disabled.

EDUCATIONAL

Some kids like to help other kids, whether it's teaching them how to read better or teaching them to swim. Tutor younger children or read to them. Volunteer at a day camp. Teach a craft at a community center.

ENVIRONMENTAL

Do you like the outdoors and care about what happens to our forests and parks? Call KAP, Kids Against Pollution. Get in touch with TREE MUSKETEERS or the Earth's Birthday Project. Contact your town's officials to see if they would like you to help clean a park. Offer to plant trees and flowers at a public place or for a neighbor.

HEALTH-RELATED

Do you like to help sick or disabled people? Some organizations, including the March of Dimes and the National Easter Seal Society, welcome kid volunteers. You can help prevent drug or alcohol abuse by joining or starting a Just Say No club at your school. Local hospitals also use volunteers. By joining the International Service Association for Health, you can make puppets that demonstrate good health habits to kids all over the world.

POLITICAL

There doesn't need to be a presidential election in the works for you to do political volunteer work. Offer to stuff envelopes for local politicians, like members of your own town council. Post flyers about your town's new fund-raising efforts or a new law. Or you and your friends could draw attention to a community problem, then get others involved in finding a solution.

SOCIAL SERVICE

To help those less fortunate, volunteer to work at a local soup kitchen. Start a campaign for food or clothes for a homeless shelter, or for needy families you hear about in the news. You can help children in other countries through UNICEF or the American Red Cross. Or you could start a project with your Scout troop, school, synagogue, or church.

Discover your own way to serve.

How Much Time Do You Have?

Many kids volunteer a few hours a week or a few days a month. Other kids spend most of their weekends and after-school hours helping their cause. Some kids donate their school vacation hours to help.

The amount of time you give to a project is up to you. Most important, be realistic about the time you'll have available. The organization you work for depends on you to be there. So before you start to volunteer, think about how much homework you have, your chores at home, and other commitments you have to your school, family, and friends.

Some types of volunteer work suit people who like structured times and hours. Other jobs are more suitable for kids who want to set up their own hours or just volunteer now and then.

SET YOUR OWN HOURS WHEN YOU OFFER TO:

- Help tutor a student.
- Assist an elderly or disabled neighbor with chores.
- Collect donations for a cause you set up yourself.

Some volunteer work is a one-shot deal. It's done once a year, or as needed. You see something that deserves immediate attention and do what you can to help.

ONE-TIME ACTIVITIES:

- Donate clothes to an organization at Christmas.
- Collect money for UNICEF at Halloween.
- Help victims of disasters—such as tornadoes, hurricanes, or floods—when they occur.

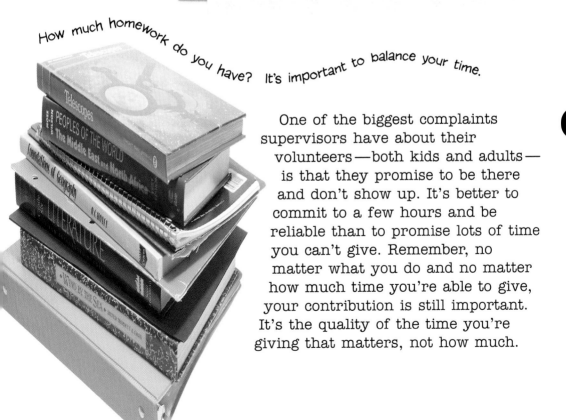

How much homework do you have? It's important to balance your time.

One of the biggest complaints supervisors have about their volunteers—both kids and adults— is that they promise to be there and don't show up. It's better to commit to a few hours and be reliable than to promise lots of time you can't give. Remember, no matter what you do and no matter how much time you're able to give, your contribution is still important. It's the quality of the time you're giving that matters, not how much.

The Scoop on Volunteer Jobs

Working at a volunteer job is very much like working at a paid job. Taking a volunteer job makes you feel grown up. It's also great experience for working at a paid job in the future. Volunteer jobs have helped many kids make career decisions.

Applying for a Volunteer Job

Applying for a volunteer job is pretty much like applying for any other job. The first contact is all up to you.

Many volunteer organizations—like local museums, animal shelters, or hospitals—can be contacted by phone. Call the phone number

Calling is the first step....

...Calling back can be the second.

listed in the phone book, give your name, and tell the person who answers that you'd like to volunteer. The person you need to talk with may be available, or he or she may need to call you back. Leave your name and phone number, and thank whomever spoke with you. Sometimes you may not talk to anyone—you'll leave your message on voice mail instead.

If you don't hear back in a few days, call back. Sometimes the person who answered may not realize that the organization has a children's division. He or she may be a part-time worker, or even a new volunteer.

Your call may not be returned as soon as you'd hoped. Maybe no one has had time to check the voice mail. If you don't get results the second time you call, have an adult make another call for you. Sometimes adults in organizations don't take kids seriously. That's unfair, but it does happen. Still, you should always be patient. One of the best ways to impress adults is by being polite.

Writing Letters

Some organizations may not have a local phone number. You can still reach them by writing a letter. Your letter should be neat, with proper spelling and punctuation. If you don't have good handwriting or printing, type your letter on a computer or have someone type it for you.

All you need to mention in your letter is that you'd like to work for the organization. The organization will send you information if they are interested in you. Make sure you include your phone number and a self-addressed, stamped envelope so that the organization can easily reply to your request.

Here's an example of a letter you might send to a volunteer organization to request further information:

Jayne Jackson
1896 Central Avenue
Durango, CO 81301
(303) 555-8037

The Plant-a-Tree Club
10010 Sycamore Street
Moose Harbor, ME 04400

Dear Plant-a-Tree Club:

I am a fifth-grader who is interested in planting trees for Plant-a-Tree in my neighborhood. Please send me information on how I can help.

I've enclosed a self-addressed, stamped envelope for your reply. I am also available by phone every day after four o'clock.

I look forward to hearing from you. Thank you for your time.

Cordially,

Jayne Jackson

Jayne Jackson

Filling Out Applications

Many volunteer organizations require that you fill out an application. Some organizations will send you an application and have you mail it back to them. Others will set up an interview and then expect you to fill out the application at that time. Either way, you need to write or print neatly so that your application is readable. But some of us don't have terrific handwriting. Here are some tips for making the neatest application possible:

- If you must fill out the application at the interview, read it over carefully a few times. Then print slowly. Have an erasable pen and eraser with you, in case you make any mistakes.

- If the organization sends the application to your home, make copies of it. Practice filling it out until you've got one that looks neat. Then send it back, or take the filled-out application with you to the interview.

Most applications ask about experience, school grades, hobbies, and interests. Since you're a kid, you may not have any job experience yet. But you probably have some hobbies or other experience related to the volunteer job.

Apply yourself from the start.

Let's say you're applying to volunteer at an animal shelter. If you have pets of your own, or you did an outstanding poster for "Pet Week," let the organization know. Ditto if you're applying to be a junior counselor at a day camp, and if you've baby-sat or helped care for younger siblings. Put that information down. Think about the organization and its focus. Then list anything you've done that might interest the hiring staff.

When you're applying for a volunteer job, it isn't the time to be secretive or modest. But be honest about what you put down. If the application asks for school grades, don't say you're an honor roll student if you normally get Cs. The organization might check. They probably don't want the smartest kid at school anyway. They want the one who'll do the most for their cause.

Highlight your accomplishments, like honors or awards. Tell about any winning teams or projects you've participated in. Mention any organizations you belong to, such as Scouts or church and synagogue youth groups.

Writing an Essay

Some organizations require an essay about why you'd like to work for them. Don't cringe. This essay won't be graded like it would be at school. The organization just wants to get to know you and find out why you'd like to be a volunteer.

An essay takes some thought, though. "Because I'd like to help people, animals or the earth" isn't specific enough. You need a definite reason for volunteering. The organization wants to know exactly why you're interested in *them*.

Here's an example of an essay you might write for an organization seeking junior library volunteers:

Why I Want to Be a Library Volunteer
by Tom Essex

I would like to be a junior library volunteer at West Ridge Library this summer, because I enjoy younger children and books.

My sister is six years old, and I read to her every day. I'm also a junior reader at Fairpark, the school I attend. I have read to the kindergartners twice a week for the past two years. They ask a lot of questions, and I am very patient with them. I also enjoy making puppets to go along with the books I read.

I would enjoy helping the children who visit the library this summer by reading aloud to them, and I'd like to help them choose books. I'd also like to teach younger kids how to make craft projects that go with the stories I read to them and the stories they read by themselves.

I'm sure being a summer library volunteer will help me grow as a person, by encouraging other children to enjoy books as much as I do.

Interviewing for a Volunteer Job

hair looks neat

clothes not wrinkled

briefcase optional

shiny shoes

Dressed for Success

Once an organization decides they're interested in you, they may ask you to come in for an interview. It's very important to make a good first impression, which begins with your appearance. You want to give the interviewer the message that you think the volunteer job is important and you'll try hard to do well. No matter what organization you are dealing with, this is not the time to wear tight print leggings, loud T-shirts, or frayed jeans. Wear clothes that are clean, neatly pressed, and tucked in.

When you arrive at the interview, let the interviewer know how glad you are to be there. The interviewer will likely discuss the organization and what you'll be doing. He or she will ask you about your experience and interests. Much of what you stated in your application or essay will be covered again in the interview.

Then, you can ask your own questions. Be thoughtful and ask questions you really want answered.

BE SURE TO ASK:
- How many years do your volunteers stay with you?
- What kinds of jobs do volunteers look for in the future?
- What schools do they go to?
- How old are the other volunteers I would be working with?
- How much experience do the other volunteers have?

When the interview is over, shake the interviewer's hand. Thank the interviewer for his or her time. Then, when you are at home, write the person a letter or note, repeating your thanks. This shows the organization that you are truly interested in them, because you've taken extra time to show it.

Hooray, You're Hired!

Getting hired for a volunteer job is an accomplishment. It means that you'll be part of a group of people working on something very important to you. Although you aren't being paid for your work, having a volunteer job is a responsibility you must take seriously. It means showing up on certain days and times for a specific number of hours. It means going to your job unless you're sick or there is an emergency. If you can't be there, you must tell the person in charge so arrangements can be made for somebody else to take your place.

At most volunteer jobs, you'll have a boss or supervisor. Dealing with a boss is a lot like cooperating with your teacher at school. Your boss might be young—in some cases, not much older than you are. Still, this person needs the same respect you would show an adult. Your boss is in charge. You'll need to listen to and follow your boss's instructions.

Volunteering means working together...

You'll also meet other kids at a volunteer job. Some of these kids will have more experience than you do. Remember that you're the new kid on the block, and let the experienced kids show you how things are done. Thank them for their help. After you've been there awhile, you can offer ideas about how things can be done better. Eventually, you'll be a part of the team, and others may even ask for your suggestions.

You'll probably make friends while working at your job, just like you would at school. You'll want to joke around or chat. But do your socializing when your duties are over for the day. It's true that you aren't paid for volunteer work, and it's often fun. Still, your duties are important. And lots of kids use references from volunteer jobs when they apply for paid jobs or for college. So you'll want to do your best.

...and making friends.

Doing It on Your Own

Some kids would prefer to do a volunteer project they've created. Some of these kids' efforts have been backed by organizations, while other kids have run projects totally by themselves. In both cases, kids have carried out their own projects with tremendous success. They've even formed their own volunteer organizations.

Make a world of difference...in small ways.

Start Small

The most successful projects start out simple and begin by focusing on a single, local issue. It may seem like a great idea to raise millions of dollars for all the starving children in the world, but your project will be more successful and easier to handle if it's local. And it will probably mean just as much to you, because you'll see the results in your own community.

Ryan Rigney started Socks Across Tennessee by collecting socks for one homeless shelter. He focused on a specific item and one organization. Later his campaign grew into a statewide, then national effort. TREE MUSKETEERS is another example of a small project that grew into a large one.

Often the projects that kids start themselves involve an issue that is close to them—like Jon Wagner-Holtz's Kids Konnected, which he started because his mom was sick. Becky Streifler wanted to help one boy with an operation, because his situation made her feel bad. These children felt that an issue affected them directly, and they found ways to deal with it in their projects.

Getting Started

For any volunteer effort you begin, you need to have a plan and a specific goal. Just saying, "I want to help the elderly," or "I'd like to clean up the city," isn't specific enough.

BEFORE YOU VOLUNTEER, DECIDE:

- **Who exactly you want to help,** or what specifically you want to change.
- **How you'll do it.** Will you ask for donations, write letters to politicians, or plan an activity, such as gathering people and materials to clean up graffiti?
- **How much time you will devote to your project,** and when you expect it to be completed.
- **Who you will be working with.** Do you want to work by yourself, with kids only, or with adults?
- **Whether or not you'll need help from an established organization.**

Finding Helpers

Some volunteer projects work out fine as individual efforts. You can do the work yourself from start to finish without any help. But for some projects, you'll need help from other people—both kids and adults.

TO FIND HELPERS, JUST ASK:

- Kids you know at your school, church, or synagogue.
- Kids in your Scout troop, Indian Guide or Campfire group.
- Your priest, rabbi, or minister. He or she may announce your project at a service and encourage congregation members to help you.
- Your teachers and principal. They may let you visit classrooms to discuss your project. Or they may even announce it at an assembly or put a notice in the school newspaper.
- Your own family. Some kids and their families do special projects together.

Making Your Project Known

Making people aware of your project is especially important if you need money to accomplish your goal. Announcements can be put up in stores, community centers, churches, schools, or synagogues. (Just ask for permission first.) You can hand out stacks of flyers to people you know, and ask those people to give some to their friends. This is called networking. It's one of the best ways to make things known. Networking also helps you find other people with common interests.

Make sure your flyers include:

- What your project is about.
- What others can do to help.
- Your name and your project's name.
- Your phone number.

GIVE A HOOT, CONTRIBUTE!

ON JULY 19TH- ASSEMBLE AT RIVERWALK PARK AT 3PM TO HELP STUDENTS FOR A CLEANER CITY CLEAN THE PARK! iF POSSiBLE, PLEASE BRiNG A FEW GARBAGE BAGS WiTH YOU.

A FREE DiNNER FOR VOLUNTEERS WiLL FOLLOW. FOOD *iNCLUDiNG VEGETARiAN OPTiONS* AND BEVERAGES WiLL BE PROViDED BY LOCAL RESTAURANTS.

For more information, contact Margot Quebec at 555-2358 or Julian Vinca at 555-4629. See You There!

Getting on TV or in the Newspaper

A great way to spread the word about your project is to get exposure in the media. This means being featured in a newspaper or on radio or television. Small broadcasting stations and community newspapers are always looking for news about local citizens. You might be especially interesting to them, because you're a kid.

Your chances of getting a story are especially good if your local paper contains a kids' news section. Part of Becky Streifler's success in raising more than $20,000 had to do with thousands of people learning about Kids Who Care from her town's local media.

Have an adult call the media to tell about your project. A local station or newspaper reporter may decide to interview you. If you're lucky, a story about your project could reach hundreds or thousands of people.

When You're in Charge

It's fun to be the one who thinks up a project and inspires other people to work with you. It makes you feel powerful and grown-up. When you're in charge, you need to use your best people and organizational skills, or your project may not work as well as you've planned. Follow these leadership tips for a successful project.

LEADERSHIP TIPS:

- **Be realistic about what you can and can't handle yourself. It's better to take on a few tasks and do them well than to take on too many responsibilities and not give them the attention they deserve.**

- **Think of other people's strengths and weaknesses. Give them jobs they're good at and would like to do.**

- **Make sure everyone feels important and has a job to do.**

- **Tell your volunteers how much you appreciate their time and talent.**

- **When your project is completed, send everyone who helped a thank-you note. Remember the people who gave donations as well as those who worked directly with you.**

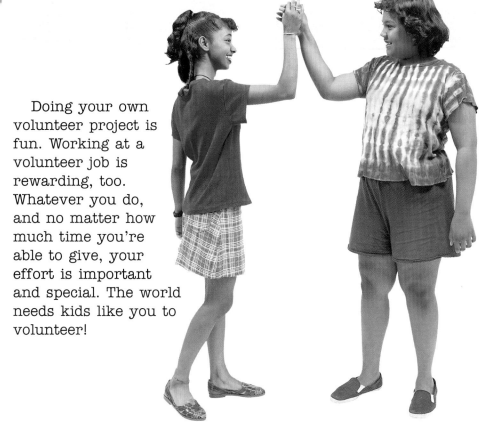

Doing your own volunteer project is fun. Working at a volunteer job is rewarding, too. Whatever you do, and no matter how much time you're able to give, your effort is important and special. The world needs kids like you to volunteer!

53

You Can Find Out More

Lots of organizations need kids to work for them. Some of them offer opportunities to work on your own. Others will encourage you to form your own local chapter of the organization.

General

Points of Light Foundation
1-800-879-5400
Refers people to volunteer organizations in their own area.

Environmental

KAP (Kids Against Pollution)
Tenakill School
275 High Street
Closter, NJ 07624
(201) 768-1352
KAP forms kids'
networks against pollution.
This organization charges a
small fee to join.

TREE MUSKETEERS
136 Main Street
El Segundo, CA 90245
1-800-473-0263 (kids' hotline)
http://www.planetopia.com/treemusk.html
*Become a member of the Council of Youth Directors,
or help with tree plantings or office work.*

Earth's Birthday Project
Packer Collegiate Institute
170 JorAlemon Street
Brooklyn, NY 11201
(718) 834-0516

Animal-Related

Leader Dogs for the Blind
1039 South Rochester Road
Rochester, MI 48063
*Volunteers raise puppies that become
leader dogs for people who are blind.*

National Audubon Society
325 Cornwall Bridge Road
Sharon, CT 06069
(860) 364-0520
*Strives to conserve and restore
natural ecosystems, focusing on
birds and other wildlife.
Volunteers may join the Audubon
Activist Network and write
letters or make phone calls in
support of environmental
protection laws.*

Health-Related

Just Say No, International
2000 Franklin
Suite 400
Oakland, CA 94612
(510) 451-6666

Kids Konnected
P. O. Box 603
Trabuco Canyon, CA 92678
(714) 589-3334
www.kidskonnected.org

March of Dimes
1275 Mamaronek Avenue
White Plains, NY 10605
(914) 997-4456
www.modimes.org
Help improve the health of babies by fundraising for the March of Dimes. Ask about the volunteer marathon programs WonderWalk and WalkMania.

Global Health Action
P. O. Box 115086
Atlanta, GA 30329
(404) 634-5748
global_health_action@ecunet.org
Youth volunteers may raise money for the Goat Project, which trains Haitian families about goat care and provides them with goats. Goats give the families milk, food, and much-needed income. Certificates of appreciation are awarded, and you can even name your goat!

Social Service

American Red Cross
8111 Gatehouse Road
Falls Church, VA 22042
(703) 206-7410
www.redcross.org
Call the youth service department to connect you to your local chapter, and find out what volunteer opportunities exist in your town. The Red Cross website offers a youth site link describing many projects available.

UNICEF
U.S. Committee for UNICEF
333 East Thirty-eighth Street
6th Floor
New York, NY 10016
1-800-FORKIDS
UNICEF strives to bring good health and hope to children in 128 countries. The organization developed Trick or Treat for UNICEF, in which volunteers can collect money at Halloween for children across the world.

Habitat For Humanity
121 Habitat Street
Americus, GA
31709-3498
(912) 924-6935
Works together with disadvantaged people to build low-cost housing. Call for information about opportunities to volunteer in your area.

Daily Bread
Carolyn North
2447 Prince Street
Berkeley, CA 94705
(707) 875-2541
*Will collect uneaten food at your school and
donate it to individuals in need. You can donate
canned goods or extra fruit or vegetables
grown in your garden. Call for more
information.*

Second Harvest
116 South Michigan Avenue
Chicago, IL 60603
(312) 263-2303
*A network of
food banks that distributes food to homeless
shelters, daycare centers, and senior citizen
centers. The organization directs volunteers to
food banks in their area.*

Contests and Awards

Some organizations give awards to kids and adults who show super volunteer efforts.

The President's Volunteer Action Awards
1737 H Street N.W.
Washington, DC 20006

Mickey Mouse Club Hall of Fame
Walt Disney MGM
P. O. Box 10200
Lake Buena Vista, FL 32838
Winners receive a trophy.

Pizza Hut Hero Award
Box 428
Wichita, KS 67201
Offers scholarships to kids under 14 who have been outstanding volunteers.

USA Make a Difference Day
(202) 223-9186
Awards outstanding volunteer projects with money.

The Hope Award
Fifth Biennial Symposium
1726 Suite C
Houston, TX 70030
Offers awards to individual kids and groups.

More Information

For More Reading

Duper, Linda Leeb. *160 Ways to Help the World: Community Service Projects for Young People.* New York: Facts on File, 1996.

Gay, Kathlyn. *Care and Share: Teenagers and Volunteerism.* New York: Julian Messner, 1977.

Gilbert, Sara. *Lend a Hand: The How, Where, and Why of Volunteering.* New York: Morrow Junior Books, 1988.

Goodman, Alan. *The Big Help Book: 365 Ways You Can Make a Difference by Volunteering.* New York: Pocket Books, 1994.

Guernsey, JoAnn Bren. *Hillary Rodham Clinton: A New Kind of First Lady.* Minneapolis: Lerner, 1993.

Henderson, Kathy. *What Would We Do without You? A Guide to Volunteer Activities for Kids.* Whitehall, VA: Betterway, 1990.

Hollender, Jeffrey and Linda Catling. *How to Make the World a Better Place: 116 Ways You Can Make a Difference.* New York: W.W. Norton, 1995.

Logan, Suzanne. *The Kids Can Help Book.* New York: Putnam, 1992.

Madama, John. *Desktop Publishing: The Art of Communication.* Minneapolis: Lerner, 1993.

Meltzer, Milton. *Who Cares? Millions Do—A Book about Altruism.* New York: Walker, 1994.

Salzman, Marian and Teresa Reisgies. *150 Ways Teens Can Make a Difference.* Princeton, N.J.: Peterson's, 1991.

Spaulding, Dean T. *Protecting Our Feathered Friends.* Minneapolis: Lerner, 1997.

Glossary

board: a group of people who control a company

cause: an aim or a principle for which people will fight, raise money, or in some other way show support

chapter: a branch of an organization

drive: a strong, organized group effort to accomplish something

fund: to give money to support something

network: a group of people who exchange information or services with one another

networking: exchanging information or services with the people you meet

recruiting: getting people to join an organization

references: people who are familiar with a person seeking a job, who may make a statement about the job applicant's character or ability

sponsor: to pay for, or to plan and carry out a project or activity

Index

About the Author

Arlene Erlbach has written more than 30 books of fiction and nonfiction for young people. Her book *Video Games* was a 1996 selection for the ALA's list of Quick Picks for Young Adults, a list of books recommended for reluctant young readers.

In addition to being an author, Ms. Erlbach is an elementary school teacher. She loves to encourage children to read and write, and she is in charge of her school's Young Authors program. Ms. Erlbach lives in Morton Grove, Illinois, with her husband, her son, a collie, and three cats.

Acknowledgments

The photographs on the following pages are reproduced with the permission of: pages 8-9 (artwork), Rick Dupré; page 22 (R. Rigney), Leroy Munsey; page 24 (Brownie troop), page 25 (President Clinton and Tara Church), TREE MUSKETEERS®; page 51, Réna Dehler.